# Hope and Healing for the Major Surgical Soul

By Dr. Timothy King

Copyright 2023 by Dr. Timothy King

All rights reserved. No part of this publication may be reproduced, stored in a retrieval system, or transmitted in any form or by any means—electronic, mechanical, photocopy, recording, or any other—except for brief quotations in printed reviews, without the express written permission from the author. Inquiries should be sent to tim@drtimking.com.

Scriptures marked (NIV) are taken from THE HOLY BIBLE, NEW INTERNATIONAL VERSION®, NIV® Copyright © 1973, 1978, 1984, 2011 by Biblica, Inc.® Used by permission. All rights reserved worldwide.

Cover photo: istockphoto.com/wirestock

ISBN: 9798856585482

# Table of Contents

| | |
|---|---:|
| Foreword | 5 |
| Dedication | 7 |
| Introduction | 9 |
| Chapter 1. A Very Bad Choice | 13 |
| Chapter 2. No Movement and No Air | 15 |
| Chapter 3. Permanent Company | 17 |
| Chapter 4. Crazy Unending Love | 21 |
| Chapter 5. The Perfect Tree | 23 |
| Chapter 6. No Busy Signal | 25 |
| Chapter 7. It All Goes Back to the Fall | 27 |
| Chapter 8. Patiently Waiting—Not! | 29 |
| Chapter 9. The Fire of Trials | 31 |
| Chapter 10. The Secret Place | 33 |
| Chapter 11. Plans Change | 35 |
| Chapter 12. Desperate for Water | 37 |
| Chapter 13. Pain Killers? | 39 |
| Chapter 14. An Eternal Flight | 41 |
| Chapter 15. Help Needed | 43 |
| Chapter 16. A Painful Move | 45 |
| Chapter 17. Just Breathe | 47 |
| Chapter 18. Bad News and Great News | 49 |

| | |
|---|---|
| Chapter 19. Godly Children | 51 |
| Chapter 20. Perfect Timing | 53 |
| Chapter 21. Hope and More Hope | 55 |
| Chapter 22. An Angel of Care | 57 |
| Chapter 23. Broken Twice | 59 |
| Chapter 24. Houston, We Have a Problem | 61 |
| Chapter 25. Slow Dancing | 65 |
| Chapter 26. A Celestial Bridge | 67 |
| Chapter 27. Come Let Us Worship | 69 |
| Chapter 28. Be Still | 71 |
| Chapter 29. The Power of Prayer | 73 |
| Chapter 30. Continued Progress | 75 |
| Chapter 31. Others Focused | 77 |
| Chapter 32. A Patient's Best Friend | 79 |
| Chapter 33. Freedom is not Free | 83 |
| Chapter 34. Where is Your Faith? | 85 |
| Chapter 35. A God Wink | 89 |
| Chapter 36. The Doctor Ordered More Prayer | 91 |
| Chapter 37. Gratitude is Healing | 93 |
| Chapter 38. We are Family | 95 |
| Chapter 39. The Perfect Model of Suffering | 97 |
| Chapter 40. Test Failed | 99 |
| Conclusion | 103 |

# Foreword

## By Dr. Knute Larson

After Tim King endured a tragedy of major proportions, he used his practical and formidable mind to write down forty personal and workable choices for anyone in pain.

This useable, yet challenging read can help anyone, especially those who are up against something that could make them bitter or run away from God.

Tim's comments will support anyone in major hurt, for his lessons are not Pollyanna, but very reachable. Tim is a realist who faces pain head on yet finds strength from above to keep going in ways all of us can adopt.

As a person and a writer, Tim is full of hope no matter what, and these lessons learned come in the form of down-to-earth guidance for our journeys.

I especially like the way each short chapter points to an identifiable strength for pain, honors our Lord and Creator as one who loves us, and makes us smile with understanding. Hope and healing indeed!

# Dedication

To my late daughter, Kaleigh Rae King (11/26/2000–08/17/2020). She held my hand all night long, slept with her forehead on the edge of the hospital bed in the intensive care unit, and asked God to spare my life. I thank God for answering the prayers of Kaleigh and so many others. Perhaps God spared my life so I could write this book.

I would also like to acknowledge Laurie Vaudrin and Stacy King for typing this book before it was sent to the editor.

# Introduction

None of us would volunteer to be involved in an accident, especially one that required major surgery. Prolific author Chuck Swindoll said that life is 10 percent what happens to us and 90 percent attitude. While frustration can lead to anger, which in turn leads to resentment, faith can lead to a peace that passes all human understanding and results in a faster recovery. I like the acronym FAITH:

**F**orgetting

**A**ll

**I**mpossibilities, and

**T**rusting

**H**im

Faith is not always easy to exercise, but it is certainly the most worthwhile thing to have in the midst of a trial.

On Wednesday, September 16, 2016, I left work early to head to my hunting property to finish some tree-stand work before the opening day of whitetail deer season the following Saturday. I ended up plummeting twenty feet to the ground, with approximately eighty-five pounds of steel ladder and tree stand coming down on top of my head. I was cognizant enough to know I had to bench press the steel tree stand away from my head. Once I hit the earth, I heard my back break and ended up shattering some vertebrae.

I blacked out for a while, but once I awoke, my adrenaline was through the roof, presumably because I knew I was severely injured and in desperate need of help.

Using only my upper body, I Army-crawled along the ground, dragging my legs and feet behind me to get to my phone, which I'd left in my side-by-side ATV. If I'd had it in my pocket, like I usually do, it could have easily bounced into the weeds when I hit the ground, and I would have needed an even greater miracle than the one I received.

Only two men would have known where I had fallen, as both of them had been to the property to help me prepare for hunting season. First, I called Mike, who installed floors for a living, and he was sometimes difficult to reach. But this time he answered immediately with his jovial personality. I, on the other hand, was struggling to speak, and it didn't take him long to realize I wasn't so jovial. He called 911, and approximately fifty minutes later, I was airlifted to a level-one trauma center where I had a six-hour surgery to repair the busted vertebrae in my lower back. While I was in the rehabilitation center, I got the idea to write this book.

In the Bible, God allowed His own people, the Israelites, to go through all kinds of pain and suffering as they wandered through the wilderness. God, the Great Physician, sent them multiple "healing salves" to ease their pain.

In this book, I will provide forty spiritual healing salves to offer hope and healing to anybody who has had major surgery, physical trauma, or illness. Each chapter contains a Principle of Truth for living, which I call a Healing Salve Principle, along with a verse from the Bible, the greatest source of encouragement and hope on earth.

I often say, "The best life lived is a life lived on principled truth." Enjoy the read.

# Chapter 1
# A Very Bad Choice

## Scripture: Psalm 91:1–16

One of my favorite principles to teach the people I work with is, "You win or lose by the way you choose." The day I fell to the earth was the day I made a bad choice to climb an unsafe tree stand. Most accidents are the result of carelessness, and mine was no exception. While I am very grateful that the surgeons were able to put me back together, I am reminded every day that I have an eight-inch titanium rod and eight screws holding my spine together.

God did not create a bunch of robots. He created human beings who have the freedom to make good or bad choices. While I made a bad choice that day, I have made good choices, as well. I have chosen to make God's Son, Jesus, the forgiver of my sins and the leader of my life. This is a giant choice with eternal consequences. I continue to choose to follow Jesus' teachings on a daily basis to the best of my ability, which has helped me be victorious here on earth.

Are you choosing to follow vain philosophies such as pop culture or the latest social media fad? After spending four decades researching the ways people live their lives, I have found the best life is one lived on principled truth. Truth comes from God alone, which He delivers to us through His Word (the Bible) as well as good reliable science.

Choosing to live under the umbrella of God's love and according to His truths protects us from many heartaches. God is not responsible for protecting us if we are careless. Many times I have introduced one of God's laws, the law of gravity, to people who come to my office, by dropping a pen to the ground. I am now writing a book that describes yours truly defying that law and falling twenty feet to the earth. Defying God's law of gravity is not a winning choice.

---

### Healing salve principle

Choose to live under the umbrella of God's protection.

# Chapter 2
# No Movement and No Air

## Scripture: Acts 17:28

Humans take so many good things for granted. It's always a healthy exercise to pause, focus, and be grateful for the good things we have. When you were born, you were totally dependent upon your mom, dad, or a caretaker to feed you, provide shelter and safety, and even change your diapers. As we grow older, we learn to do these daily activities on our own, but as the writer of Acts reminds us, we should never forget that we do not move or breathe without God's permission.

A pastor friend of mine, who used to sit across from me at breakfast, would raise his hand in front of my face and move his fingers back and forth to remind me that he does not move his fingers without God permitting him to do so. I'm not an orthopedic surgeon, nor am I a chiropractor, but I do know the spine is central to much of our movement.

After my fall I could not move my legs. As a result of my surgery, I developed a provoked pulmonary embolism (blood clot) in my lungs, and I lay in intensive care for three days and fought to do something I had done hundreds of thousands of times before—breathe! During my rehab, I had to learn how to stand again, take a step again, get in and out of a car again, and do many other things again that I took for granted.

There's an old saying that "Pride comes before a fall." Don't be prideful. Humble yourself before your Creator and recognize that you are totally dependent upon Him. Surrender to His will.

---

### Healing salve principle

Admit your total dependence upon God.

---

# Chapter 3
# Permanent Company

## Scripture: Hebrews 13:5

As a professional counselor, I am often tempted to diagnose a client with the disorder of loneliness. Of course, loneliness is not a disorder, but loneliness is real for a lot of people.

As I write this book, our world is facing a global pandemic. We have been told to isolate ourselves in quarantine. Churches and businesses have closed down, and community events have been halted. All these efforts to protect us from COVID-19 have exasperated people's feelings of loneliness.

Have you ever felt alone? I felt the loneliest I have ever felt when I was in a stadium with 40,000 people. I was sitting by myself because I could not find the people I was supposed to meet there. I rode a bus with a bunch of people, but once we arrived at the stadium, they all paired up and went off in different directions.

The day my traumatic accident occurred on that warm summer day in September, I chose to go to the woods with no one except my Golden Retriever, Kruzer. If you know anything about the hunting world, you know that dogs do not belong in the deer woods. Little did I know I would end up lying at the bottom of the tree, asking, "How long will I be out here alone?"

But was I really alone? A well-known poem called "Footprints" talks about a person walking on the beach with Jesus. When a storm, trauma, tribulation, or trial came that person's way, the writer noted there was only one set of footprints in the sand.

The poem goes on to explain that the person walking with Jesus was upset that He had left him/her alone as there was only one set of footprints. But the poem lets the reader know that Jesus had picked up the person and carried him/her to safety. So the one set of footprints was His.

I knew as I lay on the ground in the heat of the day for fifty minutes in excruciating pain that I was not alone. I prayed to the One who would pick me up and carry me through this trauma. He promises never to leave us alone.

> **Healing salve principle**
>
> You are never alone.

# Chapter 4
# Crazy Unending Love

### Scripture: Romans 8:35–39

When we go through an accident or major surgery, questions such as, "Where are you, God?" and "Why is this happening to me?" flood our minds.

All kinds of questions were running through my mind that afternoon, such as:

- "Will anybody find me?"
- "Will they be able to get me out of here?"
- "Will I see my family again?"
- "Will I hunt or play basketball or baseball again?"
- "Will I walk again?"
- "Will I survive?"

1 John 3 tells us that God is love. I have often said that when we are in difficulty, "Love wins." I have also said that "Love is the greatest motivator on earth." This God of love not only motivates us to move through our traumas, but also to love others through theirs.

While I hoped I had grown in my faith before the trauma, I knew the greatest thing (person) I had that day was the love of my Creator.

> ### Healing salve principle
>
> Remember the vast love that God has for you.

# Chapter 5
# The Perfect Tree

## Scripture: 1 Peter 2:24

When God created trees as natural resources for beauty, among other uses, He never intended them to be the cause of injury or death. God's creation was perfect. Any outdoorsman could spend countless hours looking for that perfect tree to hang a tree stand in which to harvest a whitetail buck. I often go back to the tree I fell out of, knowing it changed my life forever.

Another tree some two thousand years ago would be used to make the old rugged cross on which Jesus would be crucified to pay the penalty for our sins. That tree has a purpose behind it that can change our lives for all eternity. One songwriter wrote of that change when he penned the words, "At the cross, at the cross where I first saw the light, and the burden of my heart rolled away. It was there by faith I received my sight, and now I am happy all the day."

Focusing on that tree can make us happy in the midst of an injury; a surgery; rehab; and yes, even death. Sin entered the world as a result of mankind's choice, and it took the tree that was used to make the cross where Jesus died the cruelest death a man could ever die, to cover the penalty of our sins.

> **Healing salve principle**
>
> Meditate on the old rugged cross.

# Chapter 6
# No Busy Signal

## Scripture: Psalm 121:4

It was nothing short of a miracle that I was able to Army-crawl to reach my cell phone. My deepest fear was that I would not be able to reach anyone who would know where I fell. Only two individuals would have understood the lay of the land well enough to point the paramedics to my location. The first young man, Alex, was a teenager who had helped me hang tree stands in the same woods. The second individual, Mike, whom I mentioned previously, was in the flooring business, which meant he was sometimes difficult to reach. I called him first, and as miracles happen, he answered his phone.

Jesus is omniscient and knows our every move (including our every fall). His phone line is never busy, and He will always answer your call for help. Call upon the name of the Lord (Psalm 145:18) and many other scriptures. He is eagerly waiting for you to ask for help.

> **Healing salve principle**
>
> Call upon Jesus 24/7/365.
> He is waiting to hear from you.

# Chapter 7
# It All Goes Back to the Fall

## Scripture: Proverbs 17:22

As I was recalling the events of that traumatic day, searching for what God wanted to teach me, I told my wife again that I crawled twenty yards on my belly to get to my phone. Stacy joked as she asked, "Didn't God make the devil crawl on his belly as a serpent?" (Genesis 3:14) We both had a good laugh.

I know I have committed my share of sins, but insinuating that I was the devil himself is going a little too far. I hope you agree. But even in the midst of a trial or tribulation, it is healthy to find a way to laugh. Proverbs 17:22 tells us that laughter is good medicine for our souls.

Bad things happen to good people because of the fall (no pun intended) in the garden of Eden. That includes all illness and injury. Everything was perfect before the sin of Adam and Eve, and everything will be perfect again someday in heaven. In the meantime, while we are here on earth, we must run this race called "life."

We cannot point our fingers at Adam and Eve, for Romans 3:23 tells us that all of us are guilty of sin and miss the mark that God has set before us. Even though I had a terrible fall and a tragic injury, I'm not only walking today, but I'm running, as well.

The apostle Paul knew something about running as he said in 1 Corinthians 9:24 and Hebrews 12:1 that he runs this race of life to win the prize, not the prize earned from humans, but a reward that comes only from God once we get to heaven. Paul knew the spiritual race in life far outweighed the physical.

### Healing salve principle

Choose to laugh in the middle of the storms throughout the race called life.

# Chapter 8
# Patiently Waiting—Not!

## Scripture: Psalm 27:14

It has been said that when we pray to God, He gives us one of three answers: "yes," "no," or "wait." As if falling twenty feet out of a tree and shattering my back wasn't enough, it was eighty-five degrees that day, and I wasn't in the shade when I made it to my phone and called for help.

Because my location in the woods was so difficult to find, I waited almost an hour in the heat and in excruciating pain for help to arrive. I prayed vigorously for God to show up. One hour seemed like ten as I had time to reminisce about my fifty-four years of life.

Psalm 27:14 insists that we patiently wait, not for an ambulance, a medical helicopter, or the EMTs, but on the Physician of all physicians, the King of Kings, and Lord of Lords, the one who loves us the most. He is the one with whom I will fly away someday, not on a helicopter to a trauma hospital, but to my home in heaven.

The apostle Paul thought he was imprisoned and his life was threatened. He knew the worst thing that could happen to him was that he would be killed and enter the gates of heaven to be united with loved ones who did not survive their respective traumas. Be assured today that God hears you when you ask Him for help.

---

### Healing salve principle

Be encouraged, as God will always show up.

---

# Chapter 9
# The Fire of Trials

## Scriptures: 1 Peter 1:7 & 4:12

Trauma to or disease in our bodies is tough enough without being told we need major surgery. It can feel like putting your hand on a hot stove. The heat from the fire of the trial is painful.

A friend of mine, who is a professional tree cutter, told me that fire is one of the worst enemies of trees. He also told me that small fires called "cool" fires can be helpful for cleaning the earth's floor of leaves and sticks, leaving behind ashes that create fertile ground for seeds to grow. These small fires in the forest are important and necessary for trees to grow to be healthy.

The fiery trials in our lives are necessary for our spiritual health and growth. James, the half-brother of Jesus, encourages us in James 1:2–4 (NIV) to "Consider it pure joy, my brothers and sisters, whenever you face trials of many kinds, because you know that the testing of your faith produces perseverance. Let perseverance finish its work so that you may be mature and complete, not lacking anything."

The injury, disease, trial, and the "fire" is where the conditions are right for God to grow us and guide us into His purpose. The fire is where God grows us into spiritual maturity and opens doors for us to further His Kingdom. Choose to place your trial in the hands of God that He might achieve His purpose for His honor and your good.

### Healing salve principle

Choose joy in the midst of fiery trials.

# Chapter 10
# The Secret Place

## Scripture: Psalm 9:1–2

A myriad of emotions can run through a family member's or a close friend's mind when he/she receives word that a loved one has been in a traumatic accident and is going to need major surgery. Those who have faith in God find a secret place to cry out to Him.

I am sure that was the case with my youngest daughter, Kaleigh, who had disappeared from the home after receiving the news that I had fallen twenty feet and was badly injured. When my wife, Stacy, began to look for her, she asked my son, Kyler, if he had seen Kaleigh.

Kyler said he had indeed seen her. She had found her secret place on a bench in a memorial garden that we had made after my mom went home to be with Jesus. Kaleigh knew that is where I had spent time crying out to God as I mourned my mother's death.

Kyler stood behind Kaleigh and took a picture, knowing it would be priceless regardless of the outcome of my injuries and my impending surgery. Little did we know that my family would sit on that bench and many other secret places as we cried out to God and mourned Kaleigh Rae's death on August 17, 2020.

Do you have a secret place where you cry out to God, commune with Him, and meditate on His Word? Find your secret place and frequent it often.

---

### Healing salve principle

Find a place to be alone with God frequently.

---

# Chapter 11
# Plans Change

### Scripture: Proverbs 16:9

Have you ever made plans that did not work out the way you anticipated? It's an understatement that my plans did not work out the way I wanted them to on September 16, 2016. I had planned to finish hanging a tree stand so that I might enjoy whitetail hunting a week later. The Bible says a man makes his plans, but God has way of changing them. We could review story after story in the Bible where plans did not work out the way the Bible character intended.

Most likely your plans will not turn out exactly as you would have them. This is where the sovereign will of God enters the picture. There are no surprises in God's world as He knows exactly what is coming our way, and He has a perfect plan where there are no mistakes or accidents. Revelation 21:5 tells us that He, "God," is making all things new, and Romans 8:28 tells us that all things work together for good for those who love God and are called according to His purpose.

Neither I nor anyone who cares about me would have written this tragic chapter in the storybook of my life. Yet as a result of my negligence, God's sovereign will permitted this to happen for several reasons. One of those reasons is that I might lean on Him during this tragedy. Another might be that I would trust in Him with all my heart and lean not on my own understanding, and in all my ways acknowledge Him, knowing He will direct my path (Proverbs 3:5–6).

While it is wise to make plans, it is even wiser for us to surrender those plans to the will of God.

### Healing salve principle

Make plans but trust in God's sovereign will for your life.

# Chapter 12
# Desperate for Water

## Scripture: John 4:7–15

In the little devotional book called *The Daily Bread*, I read about how an organization called "Water is Life" developed *The Drinkable Book*. The pages of this book were used to filter out the contaminants in the water in third-world countries.

John 4:7–14 talks about the water we can drink and never thirst again. This is not a liquid water to quench a physical thirst. It quenches the desire for the things of the world and increases our desire for eternal things. The woman at the well in John 4:7–14 was desperate to know the source of this "Living Water."

After falling and breaking my back, I was desperately begging for water as I was air lifted to the trauma center. Of course, the medical professionals onboard the helicopter were not permitted to give me anything to eat or drink. I don't know that I have ever been more desperate for a cup of water.

I wonder how often I have been as desperate for the "Living Water," where I will never thirst again as Jesus told the woman at the well. King David put it succinctly when he said in Psalm 42:1 (NIV), "As the deer pants for streams of water, so my soul pants for you, my God."

Let me challenge you to become as desperate for the grace of God and His Word as I was for a cup of water while I was heading to the trauma center in that helicopter.

---

**Healing salve principle**

Drink deeply from God's Word.

---

# Chapter 13
# Pain Killers?

## Scripture: Romans 8:18

My son-in-law, Stephen, is a young man in pretty good physical shape. Unfortunately, he had to have minor back surgery. One day he reminded me of the principle the Apostle Paul points us to in Romans 8. Physical pain is a reminder for those of us who have put our faith and trust in God to put our perspective on eternal things such as our new pain-free body in heaven.

I must admit the physical pain I felt after falling twenty feet was so intense that I begged for painkillers and water on the helicopter ride while I was conscious, which of course, the medical professionals were not able to accommodate. The irony is that physically I was potentially closer to heaven than I was on earth. At that moment, however, I wasn't thinking of eternity.

While lying in the field, waiting for help, I had a mental picture of two men lifting me in a wheelchair onto a stage to speak to an audience. Now I have little glimpses into the purpose of that pain.

Pain can be a reminder of things to come. I heard a song on the radio the day I wrote this chapter that reminded me that this ol' earth is not my home. If you are experiencing any kind of pain today, whether it be physical, emotional, mental, or spiritual, God is telling you that you are still human, but as a believer in Christ, this is not your home.

---

### Healing salve principle

There is purpose in pain and suffering.

---

# Chapter 14
# An Eternal Flight

## Scripture: John 14:3

We know that one day Jesus will take us as believers on a helicopter ride to eternal bliss where there will be no pain or sorrow. We used to sing an old hymn in church called "I'll Fly Away": "I'll fly away oh glory; I'll fly away." One day we will fly to a place where we will never fall, never experience pain, never need hospitals or surgeons, never need rehab, and never get a pulmonary embolism.

Have you ever flown on an airplane? When my wife and I fly on commercial airlines, we look out the window and see the sun beaming off the clouds and always think of our loved ones who have passed from this life into heaven. No one knows the location of heaven, but we do know it is somewhere in the direction of "up."

When the helicopter lifted off on September 16, the thought crossed my mind that while my body might return to the earth, my soul, the real me, could rise to a blissful place called heaven. Make sure when your "eternal helicopter" shows up that you are ready to meet Jesus.

> ### Healing salve principle
>
> We who are in Christ have eternal security.

# Chapter 15
# Help Needed

## Scriptures: Exodus 15:26 & Proverbs 3:5–6

When the helicopter landed at the level-one trauma hospital, multiple doctors, nurses, and other professional medical staff were there to greet me. I would later meet my surgeons, my pulmonary doctors, my anesthesiologist, and even later meet my rehab doctors, occupational therapist, and physical therapist. While I am grateful to these professionals who did their respective jobs in restoring me back to health as much as possible, my hope and faith is in none of them.

King David said it so well in Psalm 46:1 (NIV): "God is our refuge and strength, an ever-present help in trouble." God promised in Isaiah 40:31 that if we wait on the

Lord, our strength will be renewed and we will soar like eagles. I sure don't run or jump the way I used to, but my faith and my spirit are soaring like an eagle because I choose to put my hope in Jesus and Him alone.

> **Healing salve principle**
>
> Help from the Great Physician and His heavenly angels is on its way.

# Chapter 16
# A Painful Move

## Scripture: Matthew 8:17

To this day, talking about the pain associated with falling and breaking my back still sends shrills up my natural, and my now-titanium, spine. The pain I felt after the fall, while being checked out by the paramedics, while being lifted onto the gurney, while being carried the distance of four football fields through the woods, while being transferred into the ambulance and then into the helicopter, etc. was excruciating!

At one point in the hospital when the staff was transferring me from the ambulance bed to another portable hospital bed, I pleaded with them to postpone the transfer until after they had given me some pain medication. Unfortunately, I lost the negotiating process and endured yet another dose of pain in the transfer from bed to bed.

The Good News for all of us, no matter how much pain we have or have not experienced, is that Jesus has been touched with our feelings of infirmity (Matthew 8:17). Jesus, too, felt excruciating pain on the cross, and He negotiated with His Heavenly Father when he said in Matthew 26:39 (NIV), "... if it is possible, may this cup be taken from me." Yet He willingly chose to endure the worst pain anyone has ever felt physically, mentally, and emotionally.

This is the essence of God's love for you and me. For God so loved the world that He willingly gave His only begotten Son (to experience pain) that whosoever believes in Him should not perish, but have everlasting life (John 3:16).

---

### Healing salve principle

Know that Jesus completely understands your pain.

# Chapter 17
# Just Breathe

## Scripture: Job 12:10

Have you ever had the wind knocked out of you, perhaps when you were playing a sport, or just experienced a hard fall to the ground? If you have (and I'm sure most of you have), you know that gasping for air can be quite scary, especially the first time it happens to you.

After my surgery, while I was still in the recovery room, my family was permitted to visit me. I was still loopy from the drugs the hospital staff had given me and still on oxygen. I was told that I said, "That sure is some good oxygen." The laughter was timely for my family as they were not prepared for what I would look like after a six-hour surgery, lying face down with my head below my heart. Air in your lungs is necessary for survival.

Genesis 2:7 tells us that God Himself breathed life into the first human being, Adam, and John 16:4–15 speaks of God being the Breath of Life. I often tell people that when the doctor cut their umbilical cords, their parents were no longer responsible for the air in their lungs. If you are alive and breathing air today, be sure of where that "good oxygen" comes from.

And wouldn't you know it? There is a worship song titled, "This is the Air I Breathe." This was the first song I sang in worship my first Sunday back to church after surgery and rehab. Breathe in as much of the "Breath of Life" as you can get, for in the beginning of your life, He was there.

> **Healing salve principle**
>
> Take a deep breath and sense the presence of Jesus' love.

# Chapter 18
# Bad News and Great News

## Scripture: John 11:25–26

Have you ever been asked, "Do you want the good news or the bad news first?" Weeks after my surgery, I noticed some pain in my left calf muscle and I was having difficulty breathing. The nature of my profession is confidential, yet on one particular day while attempting to return to work, my wife knocked on my office door. As soon as I opened the door, she introduced herself to my client as my wife and then demanded I get in the vehicle to go to the emergency room. She had a hunch that I had blood clots. She was right.

When the doctor entered the emergency room after receiving the results of the tests he'd run, he said, "Doctor King, you have a blood clot in your left calf muscle and a very large blood clot in your lung, and it could kill you." My wife and I were both very aware that I had an older biological sister who had passed away at the age of thirty-six from a blood clot in her lungs.

My wife is a woman of strong faith, yet the look on her face after the doctor had given us that bad news was one of deep worry and concern. She immediately asked the doctor what he was going to do to treat my diagnosis. He replied that his medical staff was already treating me intravenously.

None of us knows how we are going to die, but we will all die. "Just killing time" is a misconception. We don't kill time; time kills us. The diagnosis reminded me of the brevity of life. I often remind myself of the words of the song I had sung at my sister's funeral: "Only one life so soon it will pass; only what's done for Christ will last."

The end of life on earth is just the beginning for the believer. Are you ready for bad news? Are you prepared to die? Are you ready to face eternity? Someday, something will kill you, so I would encourage you to answer these questions sooner rather than later.

### Healing salve principle

For the believer in Christ Jesus, know that death is not the end but the beginning.

# Chapter 19
# Godly Children

## Scripture: Deuteronomy 6:5–9

God is a God of systems. He created the solar system, the digestive system, the circulatory system, and the family system. If one family member goes under the surgeon's knife, the entire family system is affected. After my six-hour surgery and subsequent rehab, I found myself in the intensive care unit being treated for a large pulmonary embolism in my lung.

I just read a book that reminded me of the fourth commandment, which our current culture seems to have forgotten: honor your father and mother. If you are a parent, you have probably witnessed some behaviors from your children that did not honor your position as father and mother.

As I lay in intensive care, fighting to breathe, my youngest, Kaleigh Rae, held my hand, laid her forehead on the hospital bed, and prayed for healing and continued life for her father. God obviously heard the prayers of that young lady as I am here writing this book. Kaleigh was loving and honoring her father with her actions. As the sovereignty of God would have it, a short four years later, our Kaleigh Rae would die of a pulmonary embolism at the age of nineteen.

Our three children have watched Stacy and me honor our mother and father until their dying day. The parenting principle of "More is caught than taught" was demonstrated the day I lay in intensive care, fighting for my life.

> **Healing salve principle**
>
> Modeling truth to your children will come back to you in huge ways.

# Chapter 20
# Perfect Timing

## Scripture: Proverbs 16:9

It's so easy to take simple things like walking into the bathroom for granted. Yet one day in the hospital after my surgery I had too much coffee for breakfast and had to use the bathroom in desperate fashion. So, I pushed the nurses' button on the side of my bed and waited for help. They must've been extremely busy that day because nobody came to help. Luckily someone visiting the patient next to me was able to hand me my urinal. What a relief! The nurse showed up afterward and asked if I needed to use the bathroom. My reply was, "You are a little too late."

It's a wonderful thing to know and believe that God's timing is always perfect. He is never late. He always shows up when we need Him. James 1:17 says that all good things come from above. God showed up when I was able to crawl to my side-by-side ATV, and He showed up when a busy Mike answered his phone and called 911. He promised to never leave me alone (Deuteronomy 31:6–8). And He really showed up when the surgeon told me I would have a full recovery and walk again.

God is not bound by a clock like you and I. Trust God for His perfect timing when good things as well as bad things happen.

> ### Healing salve principle
>
> Trust that God's timing is perfect. He is never late.

# Chapter 21
# Hope and More Hope

## Scripture: Proverbs 4:20–23

When the doctor came into my room and told my wife and me that I had blood clots in my leg and a massive pulmonary embolism in my lung, the look on my wife's face was asking some serious questions, such as *How will you treat it? Please tell me you have a treatment. Please tell me I am not going to lose my husband. Please tell me there is hope.*

Scripture tells us we are all born with a sickness, a disease, if you will. It's called sin, which Romans 3:10 tells us we are all guilty of. Romans 3:23 tells us the penalty for our sin is death and eternity in hell. Thankfully, just as the doctor gave my wife and me hope on that day my blood clots were treated, the Great Physician gives us hope for our sin sickness (1 John 1:9).

That hope came to this earth as a virgin-born baby, who lived a sinless life for thirty-three years, was crucified on a cross for your sins and mine, and rose from His grave on the third day after His burial. His sacrifice and subsequent victory over death provided a treatment for our sin sickness (Romans 5:8). His name is Jesus.

---

**Healing salve principle**

There is hope for healing in the name of Jesus.

---

*By Dr. Timothy King*

# Chapter 22
# An Angel of Care

## Scripture: Proverbs 31:10–31

October 31, 2016, was my last evening in the hospital after being treated for post-surgery blood clots. I usually commit to reading a Proverb a day, as there are thirty-one Proverbs and usually thirty-one days in a month. Since I had read Proverbs 31 many times, I knew what it said. But my experience in this proverb was a lot different after having gone through one of the most difficult times in my life.

Stacy has always epitomized the Proverbs 31 wife, but she was a rock of Gibraltar with her faith and care taking. Even when she was just sitting silently by my bedside, or when she was home taking care of the house and our daughters, I could feel her love and sense her prayers. After all, she was the one who knocked on my office door with that mother's intuition and said, "Get in the vehicle; we are going to the emergency room," after I had complained about my calf muscle hurting that morning. My wife of more than thirty years saved my life that day.

I don't know if you have a Proverbs 31 wife, but if you have anyone in your life who loves you as unconditionally as a human being can love and who goes above and beyond to take care of you, comfort you, and encourage you, make sure you say "thank you," not only to them but to our Lord for gracing your life with such a wonderful angel of care.

> ### Healing salve principle
> 
> Be an angel of care to someone, as you will need the favor returned.

# Chapter 23
# Broken Twice

## Scripture: Hebrews 4:15–16

A good friend once said to me that surrendering to God is something we do, but brokenness is something God brings us to. Some form of the word *broken* is mentioned 173 times in the Bible. Yes, I was broken physically, but more important, I was broken spiritually and brought face to face with the God of the universe.

I learned that God is to be revered like I had never learned before. I learned that all good things (like healthy bones and air in my lungs) come from above like I had never learned before. I learned that I am totally dependent on God for everything.

These lessons are exactly what the disciples learned in Matthew 6:9–13 when Jesus taught them to pray. The apostle Paul also knew the importance of surrendering to God's will as he said, "I die daily," speaking of surrendering his human will.

Yes, I was physically broken that day, but I was not completely broken, as I learned to lean on the strength of the Lord.

> **Healing salve principle**
>
> Surrender helps us persevere through brokenness.

# Chapter 24
# Houston, We Have a Problem

## Scripture: Deuteronomy 11:12

Three days or so after my surgery, I began my physical and occupational therapy. I will never forget the day a young female occupational therapist and a student therapist came to my room to begin teaching me how to walk again. A few days earlier, Stacy had asked me if I needed anything from home. I told her I did not want to wear those goofy hospital gowns that exposed my backside to the world, so I wanted her to bring me a pair of athletic shorts and a t-shirt. This is what I was wearing when the young therapist helped me out of bed and into the hallway for a short walk.

The older of the two therapists asked me if I wanted to go left or right out of my room and up the hallway. I replied that I wanted to go left, as that was the direction of the nurses' station and I might as well say hello. I must admit I had a death grip on the handles of the walker, trying to hold myself in an upright position.

This is when the unthinkable happened. My shorts had a drawstring that I had not tied around my waist. So, after I took about five steps, my shorts dropped to my ankles, and my shorts were all I was wearing around my mid-section. I had such a grip on the walker in fear that I was going to faceplant that I did not care who or how many people saw me. I was not letting go of those handles.

The two therapists froze and stared at one another. After a few seconds, I broke the silence and said, "Ladies, one of you can reach down and pull up my shorts, or I will continue to walk toward the nurses' station and take the risk of being arrested for indecent exposure." One of them bashfully pulled up my shorts and tied them around my waist.

Scripture tells us that nothing is hidden from the Lord. Romans 5:8 says that God sees you and me at our worst and still loves us. This is the meaning of omniscience, one of the attributes of God. It was neither my nor the therapist's intention for the people in the hallway to "catch an eye full" that day. In the same way, you may not intend God to see some of your behavior, but I promise you, He does.

There was no shame of nakedness for Adam and Eve in the beginning, and yet the Bible tells us they ran and hid out of shame after they had sinned and disobeyed God. Is there anything in your life that you would be ashamed for God to see? Pull up your shorts, tie the drawstring, and change your behavior.

> **Healing salve principle**
>
> Understanding God's omniscience leads to better behavior.

# Chapter 25
# Slow Dancing

## Scripture: 1 Peter 2:21

At the time of my accident, Stacy and I had been married for twenty-eight years. She had been a physical therapy assistant for all twenty-eight of those years. I have to admit I did not fully understand the benefits of that profession until I needed to learn how to walk again, get in and out of a car again, and walk up and down steps again.

During one treatment, the task for the day was to teach me to step forward and sideways. The young physical therapist put a belt around my waist, which I later learned was a gait belt, so she could hold on to me to make sure I did not faceplant.

She asked me to hold on to the sides of her waist for stability as she held on to the gait belt and instructed me to step left, then forward, then right, and then backward. Everything was going well until I started singing, "Slow dancing, swaying to the music." Her laughter and mine almost changed the therapeutic task to learning how to get up off the floor.

Jesus said in Psalm 27:33 that the steps of a righteous man are ordered by God. A righteous person is simply one who chooses to do the right thing. If you and I study the life of Jesus and attempt to walk in His footsteps, we will be just fine.

> ### Healing salve principle
>
> The best way to go through the minefield is in the footsteps of Jesus.

# Chapter 26
# A Celestial Bridge

### Scripture: Isaiah 40:29

Physical therapy after an orthopedic surgery can be extremely painful. So, it is good to keep in mind that old quote, "no pain, no gain." One particular day, the therapist told me my task was to go up three steps, walk across a little bridge-like apparatus, and then walk down three steps on the other side. Of course, the railings were my saving grace. I had a death grip on each side as I completed this task.

Taking those slow and methodical steps reminded me of a few truths found in the number-one bestselling book year after year, the Bible. The physical therapist was telling me when to take a step and how to take the step. In other words, she ordered my steps. The Bible tells us the steps of a person who does the right things in life are ordered by God.

The therapist told me the goal was to get over the bridge to the other side. That is the way people refer to life after death, "the other side." I believe everybody lives somewhere forever and that Jesus is the bridge between the sinful human being and eternity in heaven.

I was holding on to the railings with everything I had. What are you holding onto for stability in your life? Is it something temporal like money, position, or power? Have you put your faith and trust in God and His Word for your stability?

The staff cheered when I made it to the other side of the bridge and stepped onto the level floor. Those loved ones who have passed away and who trusted in Jesus as the forgiver of their sins and the leader of their lives while on earth will take their first steps on a celestial shore, the shores of heaven, for all eternity. The Bible tells us there will be cheering on that day, as well.

Take that step to put your faith in Jesus if you haven't already. Jesus will order the rest of your steps if you ask Him to and trust Him.

---

### Healing salve principle

Hold on to Jesus and His Word for stability in the ups and downs of life.

# Chapter 27
# Come Let Us Worship

## Scripture: Psalm 100:4

Trauma, pain, major surgery, and illness can lead to some pretty dark days if you permit it. My clients always say they don't know how to get to the other side of depression. My wife and I have had the privilege of traveling to other cities where we must cross a large bridge or a gate to enter.

As I lay in the hospital, post-surgery, and in intensive care, with the blood clot in my lung, I chose to listen to praise and worship music. In Psalm 100, King David encourages us to cross over into the presence of our Creator with an attitude of thanksgiving and to enter His presence with praise. The greatest worship songs of all time are written out of tragedy, loss, deep depression, worry, and fear.

Choose to enter God's gates of thanksgiving with praise. Can you think of anything that motivates you to praise and worship God? Days after I was released from the hospital I went to support my daughter at a Geneva College volleyball game. I entered the gymnasium in a wheelchair.

As the game began and we sang the National Anthem, I found myself praising God that I was born in America and had access to world-class medical care. I found myself praising God for my children and my family, all of whom supported me during some tough times. I found myself praising God simply for His never-ending love for me.

Shout to the Lord with thanksgiving and praise and feel His healing salve smother you.

---

### Healing salve principle

An attitude of gratitude in praise comforts our pain.

# Chapter 28
# Be Still

## Scripture: Psalm 46:10

I like to be active. My calendar is full and my tasks are many. The danger of having goals and being productive, however, is that we don't take time to be still and know God. I promise you that falling out of a tree, breaking your back, and then developing blood clots in your body will force you to be still. I would admonish you, however, to choose to be still, calm your soul, and know God without tragedy or trauma hitting your life. Psalm 46:10 (NIV) tells us to "be still, and know that I am God."

Little did I know that my family would face an even greater tragedy. As I write this chapter, we are still in pain from losing our youngest child, Kaleigh Rae King

(11/26/2000–8/17/2020). This book is dedicated to her. Every day since she went home to be with Jesus, she reminds me to be still and know God, as the words of Psalm 46:10 are penned in her handwriting on our refrigerator.

One of our family members has kindly and graciously sent us many encouraging texts containing the words of old hymns. The powerful truths contained in some of these hymns are just as relevant and even more needed in today's day and age than they have been in times past.

One of the hymns titled "Be Still, my Soul" has these words in the lyrics: "Be still, my soul: the Lord is on thy side! Bear patiently the cross of grief or pain; leave to thy God to order and provide; in every change He faithful will remain." Be still and get to know God in a deeper way and feel His healing salve.

> ### Healing salve principle
>
> Silence is truly golden when we focus on God.

# Chapter 29
# The Power of Prayer

## Scripture: Romans 8:26–34

It never ceases to amaze me how many people make God a "crisis God." They have bought into a lie that prayer is beneficial only when a tragedy hits their lives. My wife and I have often discussed how coworkers feel uncomfortable talking about spiritual things, yet they're so quick to ask for prayer when tragedy hits their lives.

It's always a wonderful thing to hear how many brothers and sisters are praying for your healing and recovery after a major illness or surgery. Research shows that those who are sick or injured and know that others are praying for them have a quicker recovery time and a more positive prognosis. I have kept the cards and notes I have received as a reminder of those brothers and sisters in the Lord who prayed for my healing.

Romans 8 tells us the Great Physician Himself prays for us according to His Father's will. I think about my roommates in the hospital who may or may not have had a home church or a group of friends who prayed for them. Romans 8:26–27 tells us the Spirit of God intercedes for us before God the Father when we don't know what to pray or how to pray.

What an awesome truth! The Holy Spirit of God and Jesus Christ mentions your name and your needs to God the Father, who hears and acts on your behalf. We are never alone as Jesus is praying for us today and every day. Sense the Spirit of God and Jesus Christ praying to the Father on your behalf, and feel His healing salve.

### Healing salve principle

Prayer equals quicker recovery time.

# Chapter 30
# Continued Progress

## Scripture: 2 Timothy 2:15

As I write this book, it has been many years since my fall, yet I continue to do exercises to maintain my flexibility and range of motion. 2 Timothy 2:15 encourages us to study to show ourselves approved unto God. Psalm 119:11 encourages us to hide the Word of God in our hearts so that we do not sin against Him. My pastor often says that Jesus makes life better and makes us better at life.

The Christian life requires ongoing work. There is no such thing as a stagnant Christian. You are either growing or you are dying. The only place *success* comes before *work* is in the dictionary.

Are you doing the work to grow in Christ? Put forth some intentional effort to spend time in God's love letter (the Bible), written to you, and to spend time talking to the Great Physician.

> **Healing salve principle**
>
> The only place *success* comes before *work* is in the dictionary. Do the work!

# Chapter 31
# Others Focused

## Scripture: Galatians 6:2

A month in the hospital and a rehab center could have become tedious and boring if I'd let it. One particular day in rehab, I asked the staff how they were doing. Rather than accepting the traditional answer of "fine," I asked them how "they" were doing.

One male nurse was honest with me. He began telling me how he was struggling with anxiety and relationship problems. I think he sensed that I cared about him as I truly did. The more I cared about him and poured into him, the less I focused on my discomfort of forty-seven staples in my back.

Galatians 6:2 tells us to bear one another's burdens and so fulfill the law of Christ. Jesus always puts the needs of others ahead of His own. He even told the disciples in Matthew 23:11 that the greatest among them would be the servant of all. He even met the needs of the thief on the cross beside Him while He was in excruciating pain Himself (see Luke 23:43).

As long as you have the energy, seek to meet the needs of others. When we were kids, we used to sing a song that spelled JOY: "Jesus, Others, and You." You will undoubtedly sense true joy when you take your eyes off yourself and serve others. Just maybe your own pain will subside.

> **Healing salve principle**
>
> Serving others minimizes your pain and sorrow.

# Chapter 32
# A Patient's Best Friend

### Scripture: James 4:8a

    Stacy and I have had a number of Golden Retrievers as part of our family. There are lots of stories about dogs performing heroic acts that drive the point home that a dog is man's best friend. Some of us are lucky enough to have family and friends who love us during difficult times, and some of us are even blessed with a family pet that does the same.

    In the six weeks following my accident, Stacy would visit me in the hospital and spend the night as often as possible. She would tell me that our Golden Retriever, Kruzer, would whimper and cry when he smelled her clothes every time she returned home from visiting me.

Finally, the doctors gave me the green light to go home. So, my wife drove me home while I sat with pillows supporting me in the front reclined seat. My son, Kyler, and my wife helped me out of the car. My children were smart enough to put Kruzer on a leash to keep him from jumping on me in the wheelchair.

I have never heard an animal cry like a human, but that is what I heard. I don't know if they were tears of joy or tears of sadness, but I choose to believe the former. John 11:35 tells us that Jesus wept out of sorrow for others. Some would argue that dogs instinctively know when somebody is hurt.

Kruzer was with me the day I broke my back. He lay with me in the sun and kept licking me on the arm and in the face. Maybe his actions were to keep me conscious. I don't know for sure, but I have a greater respect for God's creation of family pets. While I am thankful for my wife, my best friend, who walked with me through every minute of this time in my life, as well as my family and friends, I am also thankful for Kruzer, who was obviously excited to see that I was home.

Is a dog man's best friend? Again, I don't know the answer to that question, but Proverbs 18:24 tells us we can have a friend that sticks closer than a brother.

No matter what anyone else calls you, Jesus calls you His friend. I am so thankful that my friend, Jesus, promised never to leave me, nor forsake me (Hebrews 13:5b) and that He was with me every step of the way. In church, we are used to singing "What a friend we have in Jesus." Dogs may be the best friends of many men, but I am thankful I have made Jesus my best friend.

---

### Healing salve principle

Make time for your best friend, Jesus, every day.

---

# Chapter 33
# Freedom is not Free

## Scripture: 1 Corinthians 6:20

While I was still in a wheelchair, before I learned to walk again, I attended one of my daughter, McKala's, college volleyball games in Pennsylvania. I am a pretty active cheerleading dad at these sport competitions, but I had resigned myself to be less active since I was still in the wheelchair.

I had not anticipated the National Anthem being played before the start of the game. The announcer said, "All gentlemen remove your caps and those who are able to stand, please stand." My father and all of my uncles had defended our freedoms in World War II.

*I must stand* I thought. So, two friends of mine, who were also volleyball dads, took me by the arms and helped me stand, out of the utmost respect for the men and women who gave life and limb for the freedoms bestowed on the citizens of the good ol' United States of America. Freedom is not free.

John 3:16 tells us that our spiritual freedom was also not free because it cost Jesus the cruelest death on the cross. For God so loved you and me that He willingly gave His only begotten Son to die on a cross that you and I might have spiritual freedom and life eternal.

---

**Healing salve principle**

Times of suffering can remind us of those who gave their lives for our freedoms.

---

# Chapter 34
# Where is Your Faith?

## Scripture: Romans 4:18–25

I like the acronym for FAITH — Forgetting All Impossibilities and Trusting Him. The concept of faith is nothing new. Psychologists, philosophers, and others have always believed in it. The question is, where do you put your faith? Pop psychologists today would tell us to have faith in ourselves. Many put their faith in a political party or a national leader. Others put their faith in their bank accounts or their titles.

But neither my bank account, my education, nor my level of popularity mattered when I was lying with a broken back at the bottom of that tree. The only thing that mattered was my faith and trust in

God.  Proverbs 3:5–6 tells us to trust in the Lord with all our hearts and lean not on our own understanding; in all our ways and circumstances trust in God, and He will direct our paths.

Look at the faith of Abraham in Genesis 15 when God promised him that he would have a multitude of descendants.  Abraham was old and childless at the time of the promise.  If I had been in Abraham's shoes, I'm not sure whether my faith would have been in myself, in modern medicine, or whether it would have been steadfast in God.  Abraham tried on his own to overcome the obstacles to fulfilling God's promise and ended up fracturing his family, creating unnecessary dissension as a result.

Remember the Humpty-Dumpty story? Humpty-Dumpty sat on a wall; Humpty-Dumpty had a great fall. All the king's horses and all the king's men couldn't put Humpty-Dumpty together again.  Our self-sufficient attitude and all the professional human beings we surround ourselves with cannot do what only faith in God can do.

Is your faith solely in the all-powerful supernatural God of the Bible?  Romans 4:20 tells us that Abraham did not waver through unbelief regarding the promise of God, but was strengthened in his faith and gave glory to God. Choose to put your faith in our miracle-working God and feel His healing salve.

> **Healing salve principle**
>
> Faith over frustration and fear any day.

# Chapter 35
# A God Wink

## Scripture: 2 Corinthians 12:2–10

About five-and-a-half weeks after my surgery, the doctors cleared me to take an hour-and-a-half flight to Florida to spend a few days with some college friends. We try to get together once a year to reminisce about the "good ol' days."

When the five of us first met up at one of our college friends' homes, we all sat down and the conversation quickly turned to how I was feeling. I began to share how a lot of good had come out of this trial in my life. I specifically shared two devotionals in *The Daily Bread* quarterly, from September 21 and 22, 2016, that were no doubt a God wink in my healing and recovery.

As I was sharing these two devotionals, one of my friends decided to pull up October 25, 2016, on his phone as that was the day we were sitting there chatting. Wouldn't you know it? October 25 was a devotional written by a man who had lost the ability to walk. As a result, he had to use a walker, a cane, and eventually a wheelchair. His devotional was about finding joy in the midst of his pain.

He exhorted those of us who have limitations as a result of an illness or trauma to view them a gifts from God. Whether our limitations are emotional, intellectual, or physical, we are to serve Him wherever we are. Our current liabilities enable us to go about our daily activities with confidence and courage instead of self-pity.

We commit to make ourselves available to God and to glorify Him in all that we do. Choose today to be content in whatever emotional, mental, or physical state you are in as a result of your injury, knowing that in the love, providence, and sovereignty of God, this moment is where He wants you.

### Healing salve principle

See your injury as a gift instead of a liability.

# Chapter 36
# The Doctor Ordered More Prayer

## Scripture: I Thessalonians 5:17

About four weeks after my back surgery, after getting out of bed and having a cup of coffee, I decided to spend some time with the Lord. I was currently reading a book by Paul Sorge titled *Secrets of the Secret Place*. The chapter I was reading that day was titled "The Secret of Praying the Scriptures."

One of my heroes of the faith, Dr. Elmer Towns, had released a book a few years earlier titled *Praying the Proverbs*. I had not purchased his book yet, even though I was already praying the Scriptures days after my back surgery.

Sometimes, as I lay awake at night, instead of counting sheep, I would talk to the Shepherd. I would remind God that He is a present help in times of trouble (Psalm 46:1) and that He is my refuge, my hiding place, my deliverer, and my Great Physician. I found myself praying the Scriptures I had memorized as a child.

Praying the Scriptures is one of the most encouraging things we can do in times of trials.

---

**Healing salve principle**

Commit to praying the Scriptures.

---

# Chapter 37
# Gratitude is Healing

Scripture: Ephesians 5:20

As I write this chapter, I am enjoying the beauty of the fall leaves during the harvest season. The calendar is quickly approaching that Thursday in November where most of us celebrate the things we have to be thankful for by gorging ourselves on a giant feast.

Many people are scrambling around seeking the will of God for their lives. In 1 Thessalonians 5:18, the apostle Paul makes it clear that the will of God is for us to be thankful in everything. I specifically found myself thanking God for the caretakers in the hospital and the rehab center where He had strategically placed me during my recovery. It was gratifying to know that these caretakers did not look at the position simply as a job to earn a paycheck. They looked at their positions as a calling to help people who are sick and hurting.

If you are sick and hurting and you want to heal faster, have an attitude of gratitude. There are many things to be thankful for even in the midst of major surgery. Make sure you thank those you know who are called to the medical profession and view their patients through the eyes of our Creator God.

> **Healing salve principle**
>
> Choose an attitude of gratitude.

# Chapter 38
# We are Family

## Scripture: I Corinthians 12:12

The morning of my surgery, I was honored to have my family, my friends, and my pastor by my bedside. My surgeon showed up at 5:30 a.m. He kindly and professionally explained to me the surgical procedures I was about to undergo. Then he asked if I had any questions. I did not have any questions, but I did have a request. I asked him to treat me as if I was his own brother. He told me he treats all of his patients like family.

My request assumes that all people treat family well. Unfortunately, as a professional family counselor, I know this is not always the case, even among brothers and sisters in the family of God. The Scriptures tell us that all members of the family of God are important in His Kingdom. So, let's all commit to getting better at forgiving one another and resolving conflict.

> **Healing salve principle**
>
> See all God's people as valuable.

# Chapter 39
# The Perfect Model of Suffering

## Scripture: Hebrews 2:9

God did not leave us here on earth to blindly and aimlessly wander through this journey called "life." He left us a map of love called the Holy Bible full of direction to guide our every step, even in pain and suffering. Jesus, who was God incarnate, set the ultimate example of how we should approach trials, suffering, illness, and tribulation.

Jesus did not ask for the pain and suffering He endured at the end of His earthly journey. While He knew His time on earth would culminate in the most painful death anyone would ever encounter, He approached His trial asking for His Father's will to be done (Luke 22:42).

By His example, Jesus taught us to submit joyfully to any suffering that is unavoidable, to search the Word of God and apply His precepts to our individual situations, to trust Him completely through all hardships, and to remember lessons learned through our suffering.

You and I will surely do better in the midst of our trials if we choose to look at them through the lens of God and eternity.

---

### Healing salve principle

Follow the Model as you go through trials.

---

# Chapter 40
# Test Failed

## Scripture: Matthew 7:23

Before my surgery, the surgeon gave me a test to be sure I really needed it. He held my toes in a downward position and asked me to pull upward as hard as I could. The pain was excruciating. His facial expressions and body language screamed at me that I had failed the test, which he confirmed it with his words, "Surgery is inevitable!"

There is a day coming when you and I will fail all medical tests and surgery will not help us. This is the day our hearts stop beating and our lives on earth come to an end. It's called death.

Everybody lives somewhere forever. Jesus said in Hebrews 9:26 (NIV), "Just as people are destined to die once, and after that to face judgment." This is the test of all tests. On that day, some will fail to enter heaven because Jesus will tell them He never knew them.

When our lives on earth are over, the Bible says we will stand before God, and He will check another grade book, so to speak: the Book of Life. Our names will either be in it because we accepted God's Son, Jesus, into our lives as the forgiver of our sins, and the leader of our lives, or our names will be absent from the grade book because we did not accept God's Son while on earth.

If your name is written in this Book of Eternal Life, then you will be welcomed into the gates of heaven for eternity to enjoy your Creator and loved ones who died before you, who had also accepted Jesus Christ as the forgiver of their sins and the leader of their lives.

If your name is not found there, the Bible tells us you will spend eternity apart from God in a terrible place called hell. Do you know for sure today that if you were to meet death and then God Himself face to face that you would spend eternity in heaven? If you are not sure, please pray this prayer right now, and mean it with your whole heart:

> Dear Jesus, please forgive me of all I have done wrong. Forgive me of all my sins. I put my faith and trust in you and you alone. Help me to follow your teachings and your will for my life. I ask all this in your name, Jesus, Amen.

If you prayed that prayer, the Bible now calls you a child of God, and your eternity is secure. You can now live a more productive life with no fear of death. Jesus makes life better, and He makes us better at life. Please find a good Bible-believing, Bible-teaching church so that you may continue to grow in your faith.

Let another Christian brother or sister know you have prayed this prayer. Feel free to email me at tim@drtimking.com and let me know you have prayed this prayer, and I promise to pray for you as you grow in your faith.

# Conclusion

Thank you from the bottom of my heart for taking time to read this book. It continues to be my prayer that you would be encouraged in times of trials and suffering.

Feel free to reach out to me at tim@drtimking.com. You can also reach us at our website: coaching4living.com. May God richly bless you.

—Tim King